For my mum!
C. P.

For Léonie and Gaspard.
V. A.

For Marie and her pear tiramisu!
M. B.

FSC
www.fsc.org

MIX
Paper from
responsible sources
FSC® C101807

Published by Flying Eye Books, an imprint of Nobrow Ltd. 62 Great Eastern Street, London, EC2A 3QR.

ISBN: 978-1-909263-16-1

Order from: www.flyingeyebooks.com

BIG MEALS For little hands

Virginie Aladjidi
Caroline Pellissier

Illustrated by
Marion Billet

FLYING EYE BOOKS

Contents

Introduction

The kitchen is the place to give children a desire for the good things in life. Passing on recipes to the younger generation is a lovely way to exchange ideas and expertise. Cooking is very special as it brings together all the five senses – touch, smell, vision, hearing and taste. Encourage your children to touch the food and appreciate the difference between the skin of an orange and that of a fish and learn how to tell when a vegetable is ripe and ready for cooking. These recipes have been created by top French chef, Sébastien Guénard, using fresh seasonal ingredients with tips to share with your children and help them get the most from their senses. Some of the ingredients are typically found in France, but we have included some alternative ingredients in case you can't find the authentic produce!

Before You Start

The recipes in this book should be cooked with adult supervision. Children should ask for help when using sharp knives, electrical equipment, hot ovens and hobs. Make sure that everyone washes their hands and that utensils and surfaces are clean before you start cooking.

spring

apricot

egg

rocket / rugula

broad bean

mint

strawberry

baby carrots

tarragon

Red Berries

Strawberry Salad with Mint and a trickle of Lemon Juice

For 4 people
500g / 1lb fresh red strawberries • 4–5 mint leaves • ½ lemon •
50g / 2oz icing sugar •

We call 'red berries' berries such as raspberries, strawberries, red currants and also fruits that are more black than red, such as blackberries, blackcurrants and blueberries.

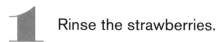

1 Rinse the strawberries.

2 Delicately remove the leaves.

3 Cut each strawberry in two lengthways. Place them in a salad bowl.

4 Gently wash the mint leaves and place on top of the strawberries.

5 Squeeze half of a lemon over the strawberries. Add the icing sugar and let marinate for thirty minutes before serving.

Super Simple Cherry Clafoutis

For 4 people
60g / 2½oz butter • 4 eggs • 125g / 4½oz caster / superfine sugar plus extra for dusting • 80g / 3¼oz plain / all purpose flour • 25cl / 8fl of milk • 250g / 9oz cherries • salt •

1 Preheat the oven to 210°C / 410°F (gas mark 7).

2 Lightly butter a medium sized baking dish and dust it with some sugar, removing the excess sugar by turning the dish upside down afterwards. Place the dish in the fridge.

3 Melt the butter (a minute in the microwave at 750D).

4 Beat the eggs together in a bowl and mix in the sugar and a pinch of salt. Sift in the flour little by little while mixing, in order to prevent lumps.

5 Add the melted butter once it has cooled and mix together. Pour in the milk and mix the batter.

6 Remove the cherry stones if you wish. Take the dish out of the fridge and put the cherries in the bottom. Pour the batter over the top and dust it with some sugar.

7 Bake for thirty minutes: 10 minutes at 180°C / 350°F (gas mark 4), then 20 minutes at 140°C / 275°F (gas mark 1) until the clafoutis top is golden and ready to eat!

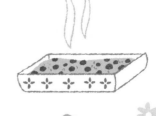

Herbs

Real Lebanese Tabbouleh

For 4 people
1 large bunch of Italian or flat-leaved parsley • 1 bunch of spring onions • 3 firm tomatoes • 1 lemon • 3 tbsp olive oil •

1 Wash the parsley and cut it up finely with scissors. Place in a salad bowl.

2 Remove the spring onions' tops and their roots. Rinse, slice very finely and sprinkle them on top of the parsley.

3 Dice the tomatoes, once washed and drop them into the salad bowl.

4 Squeeze the whole lemon on top of the tabbouleh and add three tablespoons of olive oil. Delicious with grilled sausages!

Asparagus with Goat's Cheese and Tarragon

For 4 people
500g / 1lb green asparagus' tips • 200g / 7oz soft goat's cheese •
1 bunch of tarragon • pepper • a trickle of olive oil •

What does the word 'tarragon' mean? It comes from the Latin word 'dracunculus' and the Arab word 'arkhum', which both mean 'little dragon'. It was thought that tarragon could cure snakebites as snakes were seen as 'little dragons'. That's why tarragon is often called dragon's herb to this day.

1 Lightly steam the asparagus' tips for forty minutes. Rinse them in a bowl of icy water for a few seconds, so that they keep their pretty colour!

2 Season the goat's cheese with the finely sliced tarragon, pepper and a trickle of olive oil.

3 Taste by dipping the asparagus' tips in the cheese – yummy!

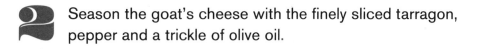

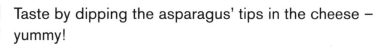

Eggs

Deviled Eggs

For 4 people

4 eggs • parsley • For the mayonnaise: 2 egg yolks • olive oil •
1 tsp of mustard • a trickle of vinegar • a pinch of salt •

1 Prepare the mayonnaise by putting the egg yolks, the teaspoon of mustard, the vinegar and the salt into a bowl. Make sure that all the ingredients are at room temperature. Whisk vigorously together and continue to whisk as you slowly add the olive oil. The mix will start to combine and the mayonnaise will soon become creamy and firm.

2 Cook four eggs in boiling water for 4 minutes.

3 Carefully drain the hot water from the eggs and pour in cold water before removing the shells.

4 Cut the eggs in half lengthwise, then remove the egg yolks with a teaspoon. Mash the egg yolks with a fork and mix them with the mayonnaise in a bowl.

5 Fill the eggs with the mayonnaise and egg yolk mixture. Put enough in so that it comes slightly over the top. Dust with finely chopped parsley – to add a touch of green to the yellow!

Chocolate Eggs

Makes 8 eggs
150g / 5oz cooking chocolate • single or light cream •
8 eggshells without the top •

*Are there chicks
in the eggs
we eat?
No, because most
of the eggs that
we buy haven't
been fertilized.
Farm eggs, on the
other hand, may
have been fertilized,
but they will still not
house a chick
because they
haven't been
incubated by
the hen.*

1. Melt the chocolate in a pan over a low heat. Stir with a wooden spoon. Add a little bit of cream. The chocolate should be soft but not burnt.

2. Place the empty shells into eggcups.

3. Pour the chocolate into the shells. Let them cool down and then put the eggcups in the fridge until the chocolate sets.

4. Once set, everyone can remove the shells of their chocolate egg and enjoy the delicious chocolate inside! It's great with some brioche. You can also decorate the eggshells with paint and ribbons to make delicious gifts!

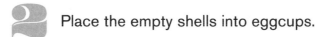

Peas

Peas 'en Jardinière' (of the garden)

For 4 people
500g / 1lb fresh-podded peas • 4 carrots • 4 potatoes • 1 onion • some butter • single light cream or Crème Fraiche • some parsley • some salt •

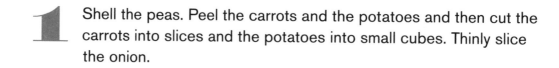

1 Shell the peas. Peel the carrots and the potatoes and then cut the carrots into slices and the potatoes into small cubes. Thinly slice the onion.

2 In a medium saucepan over a medium-high heat, cook the onions in the butter. Add the carrots and stir for five minutes until they're golden.

3 Add the potatoes and cover up the vegetables with two glasses of cold water. Add a pinch of salt. Cook over a medium-high heat for fifteen minutes. Add a glass of water while the carrots and potatoes are cooking if necessary.

4 Meanwhile, boil the peas for ten minutes in a pan full of salted boiling water.

5 Drain the peas in a kitchen sieve and place them in a dish. Add the carrots and the potatoes with a skimmer.

6 Add a little bit of cream and finely chopped parsley to season.

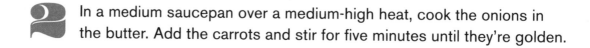

Iced Pea Soup

For 4 people
1.5kg / 3lb fresh podded peas • 1 chicken stock cube • 2 shallots •
1 tsp caster / superfine sugar • a small bunch of mint leaves • single
or light cream • salt and pepper

How to buy peas?

You can, of course, buy peas in jars or cans or frozen. But the smartest, most ecological and best way is to buy them fresh. You should pick smooth and shiny green shells and if you taste a pea, it shouldn't taste floury. To shell them, open the shell with your nail and then slide the pea out with your thumb.

1 Shell the peas.

2 Boil 1 litre of water in a pan with the chicken stock cube.

3 Slice up the shallots very finely.

4 Wash the mint leaves and chop them finely.

5 Put the peas in the pan with the shallots, the teaspoon of sugar, a pinch of salt and pepper. Cook for ten minutes.

6 Puree the pea mixture using a hand held blender while slowly adding the cream.

7 Once the soup has cooled, put it in the fridge. When the time comes to serve it, sprinkle the finely chopped mint on top.

summer

apple

peach

aubergine/
eggplant

cucumber

haricot
bean

tomato

lettuce

cherry

olive

chanterelle
mushrooms

small
peas

raspberry

melon

courgette /
zucchini

watermelon

Courgettes/Zucchinis

Courgette Beignets (or Zucchini Fritters)

For 4 people
3 small courgettes/zucchinis • For the dough: 250g/9oz plain all purpose flour •
1 tbsp olive oil • 2 tsp baking powder • 3 eggs • 10cl water • salt and pepper •

It is recommended for this recipe to use a deep fryer or a pan filled with 4 cm of boiling oil.
Take care when near hot oil and keep out of the reach of children.

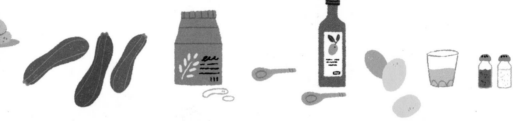

1 Wash the courgettes/zucchinis and peel them. Slice them thinly and season with fine salt and pepper (and/or *Herbes de Provence*, such as rosemary and thyme… which you can put directly into the batter).

2 Pour the flour into a mixing bowl. Form a hole in the centre and add the ingredients, in this order, stirring after each ingredient is added until smooth: the olive oil, then the baking powder, then the eggs, then a pinch of salt and then the water.

3 Pour the courgettes/zucchinis into the batter. Scoop up the batter and the courgettes/zucchinis with a ladle. Pour into the hot oil or fryer. The beignet is formed. Repeat the process all over again (you can cook up to four beignets at a time).

4 Cook for a minute. Turn the beignet over. Leave to cook for another minute or two. Remove once golden.

Tian

For 4 people
garlic • 2 onions • 8 small courgettes / zucchinis • 1 green bell pepper •
1 yellow bell pepper • 2 aubergines / eggplants • olive oil • salt and pepper •

*Courgettes
also known as
zucchinis are
very fast-growing
summer squashes.
They are easy to
grow and flourish in
desert conditions.
This makes them
a great choice for
home gardeners
looking to get the
most out of their
vegetable patch!*

1 Preheat the oven to 180°C / 350°F (gas mark 4).

2 Roughly peel the garlic cloves.

3 Wash the vegetables. Chop the onions roughly and then cut the aubergines / eggplants, the courgettes / zucchinis and the bell peppers into 5cm lengths.

4 Place all the vegetable pieces 'standing up', one after the other, in a deep round oven dish. They must be very close to each other in the dish and should be arranged to form some kind of sun when seen from above.

5 Add a pinch of salt and pepper, a trickle of olive oil (and some *Herbes de Provence*, if you wish). Put in the oven for at least an hour and a half at a medium-low heat.

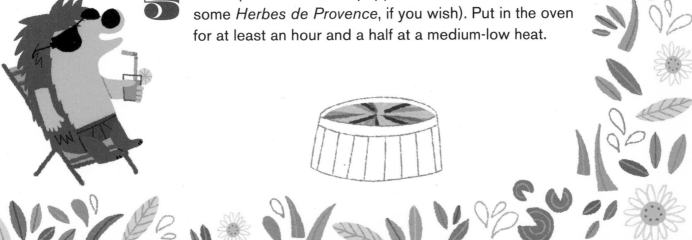

Tomatoes

Tomato and Feta Salad

For 4 people
1 tbsp olive oil • juice of ½ a lemon • 8 beautiful tomatoes •
200g / 7oz Feta cheese • ground cumin • salt and pepper •

1 In a salad bowl, drop a big tablespoon of olive oil, a large pinch of finely ground salt and the lemon juice. Add pepper.

2 Wash the tomatoes and then dice them after taking out the stalks.

3 Dice the Feta cheese.

4 Mix the tomatoes and the Feta cheese in the salad bowl. Add a little bit of cumin (you can also add garlic, shallots and *Herbes de Provence* to season).
Welcome to Greece!

BBQ Style Tomatoes

For (approximately) 4 people

10 tomatoes • olive oil • sea salt and pepper • Herbes de Provence •

There are all kinds of tomatoes: green ones, white ones, yellow ones, black ones and even stripy ones! Every possible shape of tomato exists: round, long, small or big. They say that the pineapple tomato is one of the tastiest varieties ...try them all!

1 Take the grill off of the barbecue. Heat up the barbecue.

2 Take the stalks out of the tomatoes then cut them in halves, starting from the stem down.

3 Place them on the barbecue grill. Add a trickle of olive oil on each tomato. Add some sea salt, pepper and *Herbes de Provence*.

4 Place the grill back on the barbecue and leave to cook for five to ten minutes.

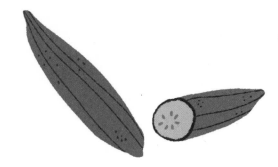

Cucumbers

Cold Cucumber Soup

For 4 people
2 cucumbers • 1 vegetable stock cube • ½ litre / ¾ pint natural yogurt • salt and pepper • Tabasco sauce, if you like it spicy! •

1 Peel the cucumbers and remove the seeds with a teaspoon.

2 Let the stock cube dissolve in ½ litre / ¾ pint of water.

3 Add the cucumbers and the yogurt to the stock and mix well.

4 Add salt and pepper and some Tabasco sauce to taste. (You can also add mint or coriander / cilantro to season.) De-li-cious and refreshing!

Cucumbers in Fromage Frais

For (approximately) 4 people
2 cucumbers • vinegar • salt • 225g / 9oz fromage frais •
½ clove of garlic • 1 tbsp olive oil • ½ lemon •

Cucumbers are so versatile! You can do everything with cucumbers: you can cook them, as a side vegetable, fry them, mash them or eat them with Béchamel sauce. You can even choose not to eat them as they can be used as a beauty product for sensitive skin!

1 Peel the cucumbers and grate them as thinly as possible. Leave them in a colander with finely ground salt and a bit of vinegar.

2 Mix the *fromage frais* with the crushed garlic, some pepper and a tablespoon of olive oil. Then squeeze half a lemon into the sauce.

3 Drain the cucumbers and mix them in the sauce you've just prepared.

Summer Fruits

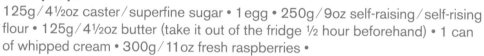

Raspberry Pie

For 4 people
125g / 4½oz caster / superfine sugar • 1 egg • 250g / 9oz self-raising / self-rising flour • 125g / 4½oz butter (take it out of the fridge ½ hour beforehand) • 1 can of whipped cream • 300g / 11oz fresh raspberries •

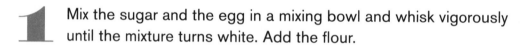

1 Mix the sugar and the egg in a mixing bowl and whisk vigorously until the mixture turns white. Add the flour.

2 Mix with your fingers! The batter should then be similar to porridge.

3 Cut the butter into small chunks. Slowly mix the batter with the butter, again mixing with your fingers!

4 Spread the pastry with your hands in a previously greased pie dish. Bake for thirty minutes at 180°C / 350°F (gas mark 4).

5 Take the pie out and let it cool down.

6 Once cool cover the base of the pie with whipped cream. Wash the raspberries and place them on top of the cream one by one. Now eat it before the bees find it!

Fruit Skewers

Makes 8 skewers
4 slices ginger bread • 1 melon • ⅛ watermelon • 250g / 9oz
fresh raspberries • 8 long skewers •

Fruits are full of vitamins. A few tips to make sure fruits keep their flavour and vitamins: eat them quickly, prepare them at the last minute and rinse them without soaking them. Fruits are quite sensitive to light and heat, so keep them cool, away from direct sunlight, but not in the fridge!

1 Cut each slice of ginger bread into six pieces.

2 Remove the skin and seeds from the watermelon and melon.

3 Cut the watermelon and the melon into 2cm×2cm cubes.

4 On each skewer, alternate between melon, watermelon, raspberry and ginger bread, always starting with the melon.

Olives

Red Mullet / Goatfish with Tapenade

For 4 people
200g / 7oz pitted black olives • 5 anchovy fillets • 3 tbsp olive oil •
1 tsp capers • 1 garlic clove • ½ lemon • 8 red mullets / goatfish fillets •

1 Blend the olives in a blender.

2 Rinse the anchovies under clear water so that they lose some of their saltiness. Add them to the olives and blend together to make the tapenade.

3 Add three large tablespoons of olive oil as well as the teaspoon of capers, the garlic clove and the juice of half a lemon in the blender.

4 Steam the red mullets / goatfish fillets for five minutes. Place them on a serving dish.

5 Spread the tapenade on each fillet. The Tian on page 21 would be the perfect accompaniment to this dish.

Pasta with Olives

For 4 people
1 courgette/zucchini • 2 tomatoes • 1 garlic clove • 250g/9oz fresh pasta • 10 pitted green olives • 10 pitted black olives • 4 tbsp olive oil • parmesan •

1 Boil some salted water.

2 Peel the courgette/zucchini. Cut it into narrow sticks (approximately 10cm in length) with a peeling knife. Cook them in a frying pan in a little bit of olive oil with finely chopped garlic. They should become translucent but not brown.

3 Wash and cut the tomatoes into small cubes.

4 Slice the olives.

5 Cook the pasta in the salted water following the instructions, then pour it into a serving dish. Add four tablespoons of olive oil.

6 Add the olives, the courgette/zucchini pieces and sprinkle the parmesan on top of the pasta.

autumn

pear

morel mushroom

field mushroom/
meadow mushroom

pumpkin

grape

celery

turnip

beetroot

fall

fig

oyster mushroom /
tree mushroom

porcino mushroom

chestnut

corn salad /
rapunzel

green
dandelion

onion

Grapes

Duck Tenderloins with Grapes

For 4 people
2 bunches of grapes • 500g / 1lb duck tenderloins • 2 tbsp balsamic vinegar • olive oil • salt and pepper •

1 Cut the grapes in two and remove the seeds. If you're feeling brave, you can also peel them – it tastes even better!

2 Cook the tenderloins in butter for two minutes each side, until they turn golden brown. Add salt and pepper and two tablespoons of balsamic vinegar just before the end.

3 Take the tenderloins off the heat and place them on a plate under a lid, so that they stay warm. Now cook the grapes for 1 or 2 minutes in the pan where you cooked the tenderloins.

4 Put the tenderloins back in the frying pan for just a few seconds. It's ready!

Grape Juice

For 4 people
1 kg / 2 lb grapes

White grapes are green and red grapes are pink or black/purple. They are one of the world's favourite fruits and grape vine roots have been in found in China that date back to before the great ice age! That's how long they've been cultivated and harvested by man to be eaten fresh, or dried to sustain people through the long winter months.

1 Get the food mill ready, and choose the plate with the tiniest holes. Place it on top of a robust mixing bowl and make sure it's stable.

2 Wash the grapes and separate each grape from the others. Place it in the food mill.

3 Grind it all up in the food mill: the seeds and the skin should remain on the top of the plate.

4 With the help of a funnel, pour the juice into a bottle.

Apples

White Pudding with Apples

For 4 people
5 apples • 1 onion • 4 white puddings or you can use pork sausages • pepper •

1 Peel the apples, cut them into quarters and remove the core. Melt the apple pieces in a pan with a little bit of water at the bottom. Add some pepper.

2 Chop the onion finely.

3 Prick some holes in the white puddings/sausages and cook them in a non-stick pan or in a pan with butter until they turn golden brown. Add the onions. Turn them over frequently.

4 Take the apples out of the pan and mash them with a fork. Add some of the onions that have been cooked with the white puddings/sausages. Serve each pudding/sausage on a bed of compote.

Apples with Speculoos

For 4 people
4 Speculoos or you can use ginger biscuits • 1 knob of butter •
1 tbsp light brown sugar • 2 apples •

*You often see
Golden Delicious,
Granny Smith,
Red Delicious,
but there are many
other different kinds
of apples with very
different tastes.
Each is special.
There are apples
to eat out of your
hand, cooking
apples and apples
to make cider
(sharp apples
whose acidity
make them
too tart to eat).*

1 Preheat the oven and take the butter out of the fridge to soften.

2 Mash the Speculoos/ginger biscuits with a wooden spoon in a mixing bowl. Add 1 tbsp of brown sugar and the knob of butter.

3 Peel the apples and cut them in half. Core the apples and place in an oven dish, flat side up.

4 Fill each apple with the mix.

5 Put in the oven for at least fifteen minutes, at 180°C/350°F (gas mark 4). Ideally, you should put this dish in the oven at the start of the meal and leave the apples in the turned off oven. They'll be just warm enough for dessert!

Pears

Poached Pears with Chocolate Sauce

For 4 people
4 pears • 80g / 3¼oz caster sugar • 1 vanilla pod • juice of ½ a lemon • ½ litre / ¾ pint vanilla ice-cream • 100g / 4oz dark chocolate • 10cl / 4 fl oz crème fraîche •

1 Peel the pears then cut in half and remove the core and seeds.

2 Boil 40cl of water in a pan with the sugar, the vanilla pod and the juice of half a lemon. Put on low-heat for ten minutes after reaching boiling point. Add the pears and leave to simmer for ten minutes.

3 Use a large spoon to remove the pears from the pan and place them on a plate to cool down. Leave the syrup in the pan.

4 Melt the dark chocolate under a very low heat in a pan. Then add a tablespoon of the cooking syrup and *crème fraîche*.

5 Before serving, place a ball of ice cream next to each pear. Pour the liquid chocolate over the pears and vanilla ice-cream.

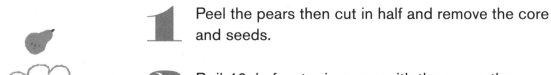

Blue Pears

For 4 people
4 pears • 100g / 4oz Bleu d'Auvergne cheese or any blue cheese • some flaked almonds •

Pears all year round. There are summer pears, autumn pears and winter pears. While the summer pears should be eaten very ripe and quickly, autumn and winter pears are picked before they're ripe (when they're ripe, they're floury), and you wait for them to ripen.

1 Preheat the oven.

2 Peel each pear, cut in half and spoon out the centre and the seeds. Cut each half into slices across the width.

3 Place the slices into four ramekins. Drop big crumbs of *Bleu d'Auvergne* cheese and dust with almonds.

4 Place each ramekin under a hot grill for five minutes. This recipe is usually served as a starter or as 'cooked cheese' just before dessert.

Cucurbitaceae

Red Kuri Squash Soup

For 4 people
¼ red kuri squash • 1 onion • ½ litre / ¾ pint milk • salt and pepper • nutmeg •

1 Wash the red kuri squash and cut into bite-size pieces without peeling it.

2 Brown the onion with the red kuri squash in a pan.

3 Pour the milk over the red kuri squash to cover. Cook at a low-medium heat, making sure that the milk doesn't boil over.

4 After twenty-five minutes, make sure that the squash is cooked by mashing it with a fork.

5 Mix with a blender and a pinch of salt and pepper. You can also add some nutmeg to season.

Pumpkin Crème Caramel/Flan

For 4 people
¼ pumpkin • 1 small pot of single/light cream • 3 eggs, beaten •
200g/7oz Gruyère cheese, grated • parsley • 1 chicken stock
cube • salt •

Pumpkins and winter squash are cucurbitaceae. You can also make gratin and soups from delicious butternut squash (which tastes like butter) or other squashes.

1 Preheat the oven.

2 Peel the pumpkin and remove its seeds. Cut into big chunks.

3 Melt the chicken stock cube in 1.5 litres/2½ pints of boiling water and add the pumpkin.

4 When it is cooked, drain it and mash it with a fork.

5 Add the beaten eggs to the mash, then the cream and a tiny pinch of salt (the chicken stock cube may already be salted).

6 Pour into an oven dish, and cover with grated Gruyère cheese. Put in the oven at 180°C/350°F (gas mark 4) for twenty minutes. When serving, add some parsley to garnish.

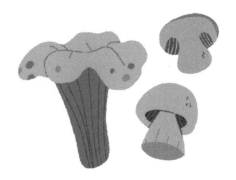

Mushrooms

Mushroom Omelette

For 4 people
250g/9oz fresh mushrooms (chanterelle or button mushrooms) •
1 tbsp olive oil • garlic • 6 eggs • 1 glass of milk • parsley • salt •

1 Wash the mushrooms and slice them. Pour a tablespoon of olive oil in a frying pan and sauté the mushrooms on a high heat. Add a bit of garlic.

2 Break the eggs into a salad bowl and beat them with a fork. Add the milk and a pinch of salt.

3 On a high heat, pour the beaten eggs over the mushrooms. Leave to cook for three minutes on a low heat. With a spatula, delicately lift the omelette once or twice while it is cooking. It should remain runny. Decorate with finely cut fresh parsley.

Ham Rolls

Makes 8 rolls (2 per person)
250g / 9oz fresh white mushrooms • tomato passata sauce •
4 slices of ham • Gruyère cheese, grated • thyme • salt •

In Ancient Egyptian times people believed that mushrooms grew by magic because of the way they could appear overnight. As such the pharaohs of Egypt decreed that mushrooms were food only for royalty, believing that they gave them super-human strength!

1 Preheat the oven.

2 Slice the mushrooms and lightly fry in some olive oil in a hot pan.

3 Turn the heat down, add the tomato passata and cook for five minutes. Add a pinch of salt and thyme to season. Turn the heat off.

4 Cut the slices of ham in two.

5 Place half a slice of ham on a plate. Once the mixture has slightly cooled pour a little of the mixture on top.

6 Roll the slice of ham and place it with the opening down. Fill the other seven ham slices in the same way.

7 Place the rolls tightly next to each other in an oven dish and cover them with the grated Gruyère cheese. Bake for 20 minutes at 180°C / 350°F (gas mark 4).

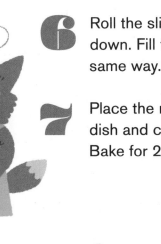

winter

banana

pineapple

brussels
sprouts

leek

endive

Spinach

Spinach and Salmon Turnover

For 4 people
500g / 1lb fresh spinach • 1 puff pastry sheet • 3 fresh salmon fillets •
1 egg yolk • salt and pepper •

1 Preheat the oven.

2 Cut the stalks off and wash the spinach leaves. Heat up a little cooking oil in a frying plan and sweat the spinach leaves for two to three minutes after adding salt and pepper to them. Drain them in a sieve.

3 Lay down or unroll the puff pastry in an oven dish.

4 Place the spinach on one half of the puff pastry.

5 Place the salmon on the same side as the spinach in the dish.

6 Close the pastry on itself. Crimp the edges using a fork and a little water to make the top and the bottom of the pastry stick together well! Brush the pastry with a lightly beaten egg yolk. Cook for 25 minutes at 150°C/300°F (gas mark 2). A tasty golden turnover – perfect for sharing!

Spinach Salad

For 4 people
250g / 9oz baby spinach (small leaves) • a handful of rocket / rugula •
50g / 2oz lardons • ½ tsp mustard • 2 tsp olive oil • 1 tsp vinegar •
salt and pepper •

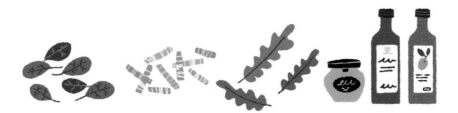

*Does spinach
make you stronger?
No, but it aids good
eyesight! Contrary
to popular belief
spinach isn't the
food richest in iron.
There is more iron
in lentils and beans.
But it's still very
good for your
health as it contains
lots of fibre and
plenty of vitamins.*

1 Wash and drain the spinach and the rocket.

2 Make the salad dressing by mixing together half
a teaspoon of mustard, two teaspoons of olive oil
and one teaspoon of vinegar, with salt and pepper.

3 Cook the lardons in a frying pan. Place the spinach
and the rocket in a salad bowl, add the lardons and
pour the salad dressing on top. Mix gently.

Oranges

Orange Soup

For 4 people
1.5kg / 3 lb oranges • 350g / 12oz pink cooked prawns • 1 small bunch of chives • salt and pepper •

1 Shell the prawns.

2 Squeeze the oranges and collect the juice.

3 Gently cook together the prawns and the orange juice in a pan over a low-medium heat. Turn off the heat before boiling point.

4 In the meantime wash, dry and finely cut the chives. Add it to the soup before serving with salt and a lot of pepper.

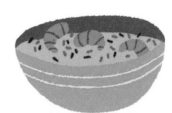

Orange Cake

For 4 people

115g / 4¼oz butter • 115g / 4¼oz caster / superfine sugar • 2 eggs • 115g / 4¼oz self-raising / self-rising flour • 1 tsp baking powder • juice of 1 orange • juice of 1 lemon • zest of 1 orange, finely grated •

An orange in my stocking. Today we are used to drinking orange juice regularly, but it's only been widely available for about 60 years. Before, oranges were so rare and precious that they were given to good children as a Christmas present.

1 Preheat the oven.

2 Work the butter in a bowl until it turns soft.

3 Then add the sugar and the two eggs little by little while mixing.

4 Add the flour, orange zest, orange juice, lemon juice, and then the teaspoon of baking powder and mix.

5 Pour in a dish previously greased with butter. Cook for thirty minutes at 180°C / 350°F (gas mark 4). You can cover the cake with melted chocolate for that extra touch of sweetness!

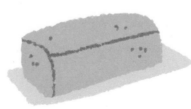

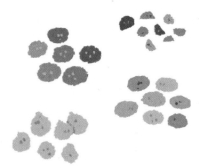

Winter Seeds

Warm Lentil Salad

For 4 people

150g/5oz green lentils (1 cup) • 2 carrots • 1 bouquet garni
(a bunch of thyme, parsley, and tarragon) • 1 onion • 100g/4oz
lardons • 4 eggs • salt and pepper • balsamic vinegar •

1 Cook the lentils for twenty minutes in one litre of cold salted water, with the carrots cut in slices, the onion cut in two and the bouquet garni.

2 Brown the lardons in a frying pan for 10 minutes.

3 Boil some water. When it's boiling, delicately put the eggs in the water one by one with a big spoon. Leave them to cook for six minutes.

4 Take the eggs out and immerse them in cold water. Shell them very gently: they are soft-boiled so the white is cooked, but the yolk is still runny.

5 On each plate, serve the lentils (drain them first if needed) and the carrots and place the grilled lardons on top. Place the egg in the centre of the plate and season with salt and pepper. Serve while it's still warm. Everyone can add a trickle of balsamic vinegar on top of the egg!

Potage Saint-Germain

For 4 people
5 tbsp split peas • ½ onion • 1 bay leaf • 2 tbsp crème fraîche •
salt and pepper •

1 Cook five tablespoons of split peas, half of a onion, the bay leaf and some salt and pepper together in boiling water for 50 minutes.

2 When the lentils are cooked, remove the bay leaf and mix in two tablespoons of *crème fraîche*. Serve quickly, Potage Saint-Germain is best served hot.

What is a split pea? It is a dried pea! We rarely eat split peas nowadays but in the Middle Ages they were a very common dish often cooked with lard. It's a food rich in protein and easily stored.

Bananas

Banana Crumble in Ramekins

For 8 ramekins
2 big bananas • 100g/4oz cooking chocolate • 40g/1½oz plain / all purpose flour • 50g/2oz ground almonds • 100g/4oz brown sugar • 100g/4oz butter, at room temperature •

1. Preheat the oven.

2. Cut the bananas into small pieces.

3. Grate the cooking chocolate into a bowl.

4. Place the bananas and the grated chocolate at the bottom of the ramekins.

5. Make the crumble by mixing the flour, ground almonds, brown sugar and the butter. You'll get a mixture that feels like sand.

6. Pour the crumble mixture on the bananas. Bake in the oven for twenty minutes.

7. Serve with a scoop of vanilla ice-cream.

Banana Fondue

For 4 people
4 bananas • 16 squares of cooking chocolate • 8 tsp of runny honey •

The bananas that we buy are … French! They've been grown since the 18th century in Martinique and Guadeloupe on banana trees – a giant plant. The bananas have to travel 7000km, via airplane, to reach us! Not very eco-friendly!

1 Preheat the oven.

2 Cut four rectangles out of baking foil, each slightly larger than the banana it will wrap.

3 Cut the bananas in two, lengthways.

4 Place your bananas halves next to each other on a sheet of baking foil. Place on each half banana two squares of chocolate and a teaspoon of honey. Wrap the banana in the baking foil.

5 Bake on a wire rack in the oven for ten minutes at 180°C / 350°F (gas mark 4). Take them out and carefully open the baking foil. Let them cool for 5 minutes before eating.

Carrots

Blanquette de Veau

For 4 people

1kg / 2¼lb veal (shoulder or breast) • 2 tbsp flour • 25cl / 8fl oz white wine (In France they use, but you don't have to) • 1 vegetable stock cube • 2 carrots • 200g / 7oz mushrooms • 1 onion • 1 small pot of single / light cream • 1 egg yolk • the juice of 1 lemon • sea salt •

1 Brown the meat in butter in a casserole dish.

2 Sprinkle with the two tablespoons of flour. Mix well, then add three glasses of water and keep mixing.

3 Add the wine (if using), the stock cube and extra water to just cover the meat. Simmer on a low heat for one hour.

4 Add the carrots, mushrooms and onions cut into small pieces and leave to simmer for a further 30 minutes on a medium heat.

5 In a bowl, mix the cream, egg yolk and lemon juice. Take the meat out and place on a serving dish. Combine the cream mixture with the stock mixture and pour the sauce immediately over the meat.

Carrot Cake

For 4 people
2 eggs • 100g / 4oz light brown sugar • 200g / 7oz self-raising /
self-rising flour, sieved • 125g / 4½oz butter • 1 tsp of baking powder •
2 medium size carrots • 3 pinches of cinnamon •

What are carrots good for? Carrots are full of… carotene, a form of vitamin A that acts against cells aging. Whoever eats them can be confident they will have pink and youthful skin. And as carrots help digestion, thanks to their high level of fibre, people who eat them don't have stomach ache… and are nicer as a result! Let's all eat carrots!

1 Preheat the oven.

2 Whisk the eggs and sugar together vigorously.

3 Add the sieved flour little by little.

4 Melt the butter and pour it little by little into the dough, then add the cinnamon and the teaspoon of baking powder while still mixing.

5 Peel, wash and grate the carrots. Add them to the mixture.

6 Pour into a baking tray and bake in the oven for 1 hour at 150°C / 300°F (gas mark 2).

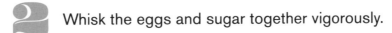